PROPER FUNDAMENTALS
FOR SNARE DRUM AND DRUM SET

PROPER FUNDAMENTALS
FOR SNARE DRUM AND DRUM SET

By JOSEPH BONVILLE

PROPER FUNDAMENTALS FOR SNARE DRUM AND DRUM SET

iUniverse books may be ordered through booksellers or by contacting:

iUniverse
1663 Liberty Drive
Bloomington, IN 47403
www.iuniverse.com
1-800-Authors (1-800-288-4677)

Because of the dynamic nature of the Internet, any web addresses or links contained in this book may have changed since publication and may no longer be valid. The views expressed in this work are solely those of the author and do not necessarily reflect the views of the publisher, and the publisher hereby disclaims any responsibility for them.

Any people depicted in stock imagery provided by Thinkstock are models, and such images are being used for illustrative purposes only. Certain stock imagery © Thinkstock.

ISBN: 978-1-4917-2509-2 (sc)
ISBN: 978-1-4917-2510-8 (e)

Library of Congress Control Number: 2014902598

Print information available on the last page.

iUniverse rev. date: 08/09/2016

PROPER FUNDAMENTALS FOR SNARE DRUM

TABLE OF CONTENTS

First Things First

Proper technique is required for making a good sound on any instrument. Proper technique ensures that your playing will continue to improve with practice. *"Practice Makes Better."*

Our guide for proper technique is Put, Place, Point. We will refer to this as *"The Three Ps."*

The first P is <u>Put</u> the stick on the first joint of your index finger and hold it with your thumb.
Find a good balance point on the stick, about two-thirds the distance from the tip.

The second P is <u>Place</u> your other fingers around the stick.
Your fingers should be placing the stick into the palm of your hand.

The third P is <u>Point</u> your index finger to the floor.

Important Checkpoints:
1. When you remove your index finger or thumb you should not drop the stick.
2. When your index finger is pointing down to the floor you will not grab the stick.
3. Your middle, ring, and pinky fingers are doing the actual holding. Think of the thumb and index finger as a guide not a grip.

We play the drum using the same hand and wrist action that we use when dribbling a basketball. If we just let the basketball fall from our hand it will not bounce back high enough to meet our hand; so when we dribble a basketball we are actually "throwing" it at the floor to make it bounce all the way back up to our hand. We use this same action to play the drum.

Think of bouncing the stick off the drum head the way you bounce a ball off the floor.
Get enough rebound to bring the stick right back to where you started.

Keep the Three Ps Rule in mind as you bounce the stick off of the drum.
I highly recommend practicing in front of a mirror to check on The Three Ps.

"The Goal is to Create A Correct Habit."

You will see this quote often throughout this book. It means to concentrate on doing the work at hand as well as you can. Don't be concerned with how fast you can play; create a good habit of proper technique and speed will come with practice.

The Studies at the end of each lesson don't have assigned tempo markings.
Play them at a comfortable tempo and increase it as you know the music better.

This book is not meant to be used as a page by page workbook; the teacher should use the chapters as the student is ready for the new techniques. Assigning work in two or more chapters at the same time should not be unusual. Each chapter is a "Proper Fundamental."

Joseph Bonville 2016

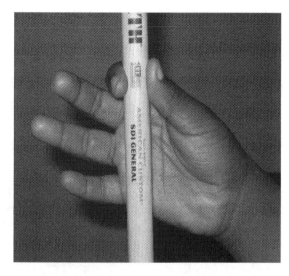

PUT THE STICK ON THE FIRST JOINT OF YOUR INDEX FINGER.

HOLD IT WITH YOUR THUMB.

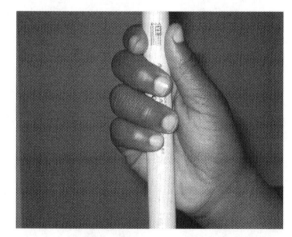

PLACE THE STICK INTO THE PALM OF YOUR HAND.

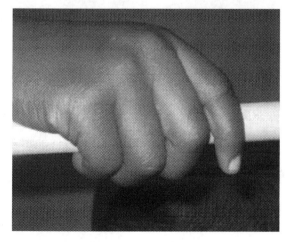

POINT YOUR INDEX FINGER TO THE FLOOR.

Basic Rules of Rhythm

The <u>Time Signature</u> tells us the two things we need to know to play the rhythms:
The <u>top number</u> tells us how many beats are in a measure.
The <u>bottom number</u> tells us what kind of note gets <u>one</u> beat.
Think of the bottom number as the denominator in a fraction which has a numerator of 1.
That fraction (a quarter, an eighth, a half, etc.) is the note that gets one beat.

four beats in a measure   three beats in a measure   two beats in a measure   six beats in a measure
quarter note gets one beat   quarter note gets one beat   half note gets one beat   eighth note gets one beat

Whole Rest   Dotted Half Rest   Whole Rest   Dotted Half Rest

Whole Note   Dotted Half Note   Whole Note   Dotted Half Note

Lesson One
Quarter Notes and Rests

These symbols are called **quarter notes.** Count 1-2-3-4 and play the drum on each note.

These symbols are called **rests.** Count 1-2-3-4 and for each rest do not play the drum.

When we see a note, we play the drum. When we see a rest, we don't play the drum;
BUT WE ALWAYS COUNT!!!

Count 1-2-3-4 for each measure. When you see a note, play the drum. When you see a rest, don't play.

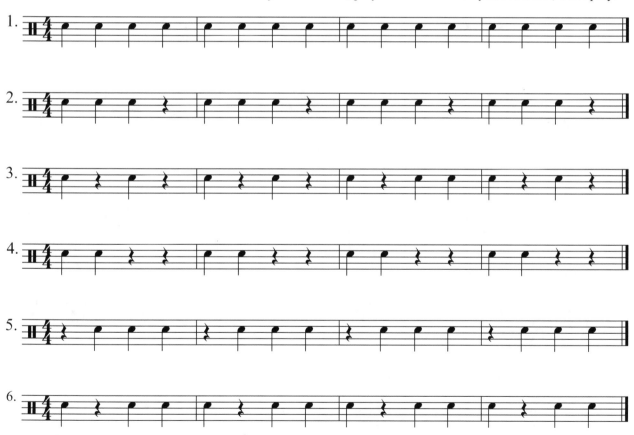

Remember that a note tells us to make a sound; a rest tells us to be silent.
Counting out loud and following The Three Ps are the most important things
to do when you practice.

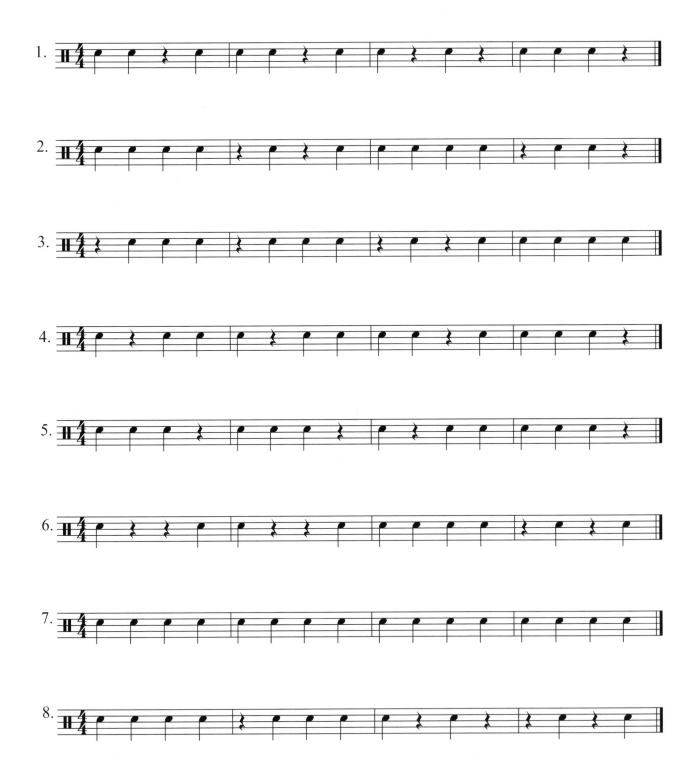

Lesson Two
Introducing The Eighth Note and Eighth Rest

An eighth note has half the value of a quarter note. Two eighth notes can be played in the space of one quarter note. Make sure to keep the sounds even! Keeping your right* hand on the beat will produce the most musical sound.

We tie eighth notes like this, or this, for convenience.

The eighth rest shows us to not make a sound (<u>but we always count</u>).

Be sure to count out loud!

Reading rhythms is easier when the notes and rests are linked this way:

*My apologies to left-handed students. Please reverse the stickings.

Study Number 1

R   R   R L R L

Go to the next line

This double bar means to stop

Study Number 2

Study Number 3

R L   L R L R

Be sure to count out loud.
Remember the Three Ps.
Play these Studies at a comfortable tempo and volume.
Keep your right hand on the beat and keep your sounds even.

Lesson Three
Introducing New Time Signatures

Remember that the top number tells us how many beats are in a measure;
the bottom number tells us what kind of note gets one beat.

Be sure to count out loud.

Study Number 1

Study Number 2

*Click the sticks together

Be sure to count out loud.

Play each Study at a moderate tempo and volume.

Increase the tempo when you are comfortable.

Start the measure (whenever possible) with your dominant hand. This will give you a more consistent sound and help your counting.

The Goal is to Create a Correct Habit.

Study Number 3

Study Number 4

Click sticks

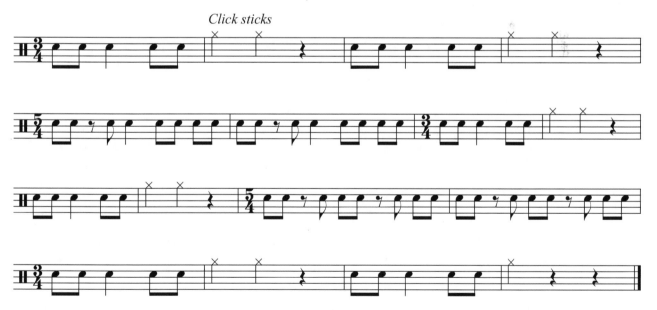

Be sure to count out loud.

Lesson Four
Introducing New Time Signatures
Introducing Dotted Notes and Triplets

Remember that the top number tells us <u>how many beats are in a measure</u>;
the bottom number tells us <u>what kind of note gets one beat.</u>
Be sure to count out loud.
Remember the Three Ps.

The dot after a note is worth half the value of the note. Add this number to the note value and the __total__ will give you the value of the dotted note. Exercises one and two will sound the same.

Three eighth notes tied together with a number 3 indicates a <u>triplet.</u> Since written music is mathematical, any time that we see a number with a group of notes it means that we are, in effect, "breaking the rules." In this case the number 3 tells us to play three eighth notes in the space where two normally exist.
Exercises 3 and 4 will sound alike.

Study Number 1

Study Number 2

Left Hand on Drum
Right Hand on Rim
Snares Off

Play these studies at a moderate tempo and volume. Increase the tempo when you are comfortable.

Introducing the "Cut Time" Signature *(al la breve signature)*

Al la breve refers to the time signature itself. Translated it means, "According to the breve (half note)"
Alla breve refers to how the music is played, that is, the half note gets one beat.

Cut Time is often notated with this symbol.

Be sure to count out loud.
Play at a moderate tempo and volume.
Start each measure with your dominant hand. The Goal is to Create a Correct Habit.

Lesson Five

Introducing dynamic markings, accents. repeat signs, and 1st and 2nd Endings

Repeat signs are "music shorthand." They indicate an area of music that is repeated.

Create a correct habit of obeying the rules for repeat signs. Don't skip them!

Dynamic markings indicate the volume level at which the music is played.

Volume is determined by stick speed and height. Raising the stick will raise the volume.

An accent mark indicates a note that is played louder, usually one dynamic mark louder.

p   This letter indicates ***piano,*** the Italian word for soft. Keep your sticks close to the drum.
Think of whispering for your volume level.

*this symbol is a repeat sign.
play the measures inside
the signs again.

mp   These letters indicate ***mezzo piano***, Italian for medium soft. Raise your sticks a little higher.
Think of quiet talking for your volume level.

mf   These letters indicate ***mezzo forte***, Italian for medium loud. Raise your sticks a little higher.
Think of normal talking for your volume level.

f   This letter indicates ***forte***, Italian for loud. Raise your sticks a little higher.
Think of loud talking for your volume level.

These markings are **accents**. Raise your stick to accent a note.

It is important that we discuss the kinds of strokes we use to play the dynamics, and more importantly, the kinds of strokes we use when *changing* dynamics. We will discuss complete (full) strokes, down strokes, and up strokes.

A complete (full) stroke is one that starts at the proper height to produce the indicated dynamic level and returns to that height after playing the note.

A down stroke is one that starts at the proper height to produce the indicated dynamic level but stays down to produce a softer dynamic level from the following note.

An up stroke is one that starts close to the drum to produce a soft dynamic level and returns to the proper position to produce a louder dynamic level from the following note.

Play this exercise with complete (full) alternating strokes. Start each measure with the appropriate stick height and return to that height. *Create a Correct Habit.*

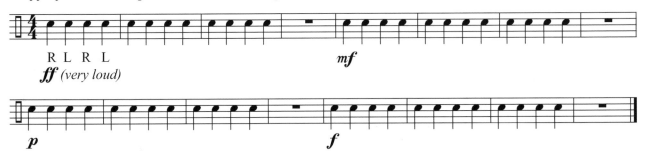

Play this exercise with a combination of down strokes and up strokes.
Take your time. *The Goal is to Create a Correct Habit.*

Play this exercise using complete (full), down, and up strokes.
Down and up strokes are marked.

Repeat this exercise many times, working for speed and dynamic accuracy.

This symbol indicates "Common Time," which is 4/4 time.

Study Number 1

you will skip the first ending and go to
the second ending after making the repeat.

Study Number 2

Be sure to count out loud. Remember to use the Full, Up, and Down Strokes when necessary.

Lesson Six
Introducing 16th notes

16th notes are half the size of 8th notes. Four 16th notes will fit evenly into one quarter note.
Be sure to count out loud
Play each line at different dynamic levels

Study Number 1

this is a crescendo mark. It means to gradually get louder.

this is a decrescendo mark. It means to gradually get softer.

Study Number 2

Lesson Seven
Introducing The Flam Rudiments

The flam is our way of giving a little more breadth to a quarter note.
We play a "grace note" just before the quarter note. Since the grace note is to be played softly,
keep it close to the drum. The quarter note will be at the height determined by the dynamic level.
This is the "set" position. To play a flam, "switch" hand positions, moving <u>both hands at the
same time</u>. You will make a "f**LAM**" sound. Your hands will then be "set" for the next flam.
The hand that plays the grace note will play an up stroke. The other hand plays a down stroke.

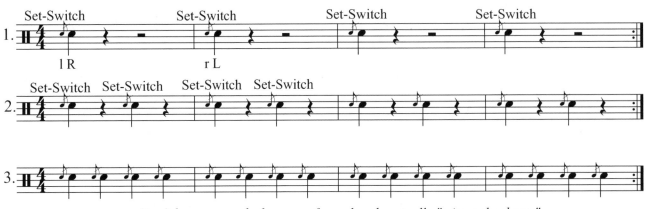

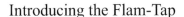

Don't be concerned when one of your hands actually "misses the drum."
This will happen as you are working to create a correct habit of set-switch!

Introducing the Flam-Tap

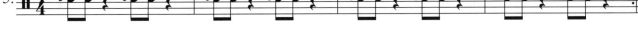

Play these exercises at different dynamic levels and in rudimental (alternating) style.

Study Number 1

Be sure to use your Up, Down, and Full Strokes to create the proper sounds.

Study Number 2
to be played in concert style

Study Number 3
To be played in Rudimental Style

The Remaining Flam Rudiments

Flam Accent

Flamacue

Flam Paradiddle

Single Flammed Mill

Flam Paradiddle-diddle

Pataflafla

Swiss Army Triplet

Inverted Flam Tap

Flam Drag

Lesson Eight
Technique: "The General Rule For Sticking"

The first rule of performance is to make the best sound possible. In regard to snare drum performance, making the most consistently even sound is our goal. Using your right hand (again, my apologies to left-handers) on all strong beats will help us to achieve that goal. For example, playing quarter notes at a slow to moderate tempo will sound best if played with one hand. For example:

The same is true for eighth notes:

The Left Hand will play the weaker parts of the beat:

The General Rule For Sticking is based on this pattern:

This is the sticking used to provide the best sound.

Exercises based on The General Rule For Sticking (GRFS)

You will find that using the GRFS will give you the best sound on all percussion instruments.

The Goal Is To Create A Correct Habit

21

Study Number 1

Study Number 2

Be sure to use The General Rule For Sticking and proper stick height for dynamics.
Play these studies carefully. Count out loud.
Remember the Three Ps.

The Goal is to Create A Correct Habit

Study Number 3

D.S. al Coda (Dal Segno al Coda) means "from the sign to the Coda" (ending).

Lesson Nine
Introducing Single Stroke and Paradiddle Rudiments
One of the very best ways to practice Up, Down, and Full Strokes is to learn and practice the Rudiments.

The Single Stroke Roll

Play this rudiment as evenly as possible at all speeds and dynamics.

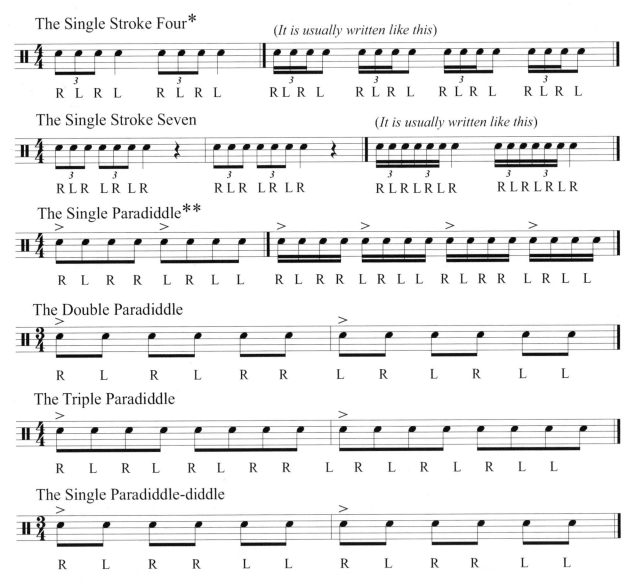

The Single Stroke Four*   *(It is usually written like this)*

The Single Stroke Seven   *(It is usually written like this)*

The Single Paradiddle**

The Double Paradiddle

The Triple Paradiddle

The Single Paradiddle-diddle

*The number 3 under the eighth notes means to play three even notes in the space where there would normally be two even notes. Since rhythmic notation is mathematical, a numeral always indicates that we are "breaking the time signature rules."

**A "diddle" is two consecutive notes played with the same hand.

Study Number 1

Lesson Ten
The Roll

We do not produce a sustained sound on the percussion instruments the way that other families of instruments do; we don't use our breath or draw a bow across strings. Since the instrument is played by striking it, we must use a rapid series of strikes to sustain a sound. We call this sustained sound a "roll." It is our goal to imitate (as best we can) the sustained sounds of brass and woodwind instruments. To that end we must produce the most musical striking possible.

There are three types of rolls: single stroke, closed (double stroke and triple stroke), and the multiple bounce (buzz) roll.

The single stroke roll is just that; a rapid series of single strokes. Developing a good single stroke roll is necessary for sustaining a sound on marimba, xylophone, timpani, and tom-toms.

The closed roll (used in rudimental playing) is produced by a stroke and a single rebound. The goal is to make the rebound sound as strong as the stroke. Each stroke makes a "bubba" sound. The triple stroke roll is a stroke followed by two rebounds. Again, the goal is to have them sound the same.

The multiple bounce (buzz) roll (used in band and orchestral snare drumming) involves each stroke producing as many even bounces as possible before the next stroke is played. Each stroke makes a "bzzzzzz" sound.

The following exercises are to prepare you for making the best sustained sounds (roll) possible.
The Buzz Roll Exercise
Important points to remember:
1. The Three Ps (Put, Place, Point)
2. Don't try to correct a bad stroke immediately. The stroke itself is the focal point of the exercise. Make the next stroke better. *The Goal is to Create A Correct Habit.*
3. Count out loud and stay relaxed. Leave the stick on the drum head as long as possible until the next stroke.
4. Don't move to the next exercise until you are producing a good sound with each hand.

Your buzzes should now connect, even at this slow tempo.

Notice that you don't need to use fast strokes to play a good buzz roll.

26

Our indication to play a roll comes from this form of rhythmic shorthand:

A single slash means to play two eighth notes.   It is played this way.

A double slash means four sixteenths.   It is played this way.

A triple slash means to play thirty-second notes.

We play 32nd notes by double bouncing 16th notes.

R   L   R   L   R R L L R R L L   R   L   R   L   R R L L R R L L

Strictly speaking, a roll indicated by three slashes is a double-stroke (open) roll.

Exercises To Develop The Buzz Roll

Buzz the 16th Notes

1.

RL RL R   R LRL R   R LRL R   R LRL R   RLRL R   R LRL R   R LRL R   R LRL R

2.

(These four measures should sound the same.)   *All rolls are usually written this way.*
It is up to us to interpret the style;
Single, Double, or Buzz Stroke.

This marking always indicates a buzz.

3.

RLRL R   RLRL R   RLRL R   RLRL R

(These four measures should sound the same.)

The two most difficult things to do with a roll are starting it and stopping it. Be careful to not accent the beginning or the end of a roll, unless the music calls for it.

4. RL RL   RL R L   RL RL   R LRL   RL R L   R L RL   RLRL   RLRL

5. RLRL RLR RLRL RLR   RLRL RLR RLRL RLR   RLRL RLR RLRL RLR

6. RL RL   RL RL   RL RL   RL RL   RLRLRLRL RLRLRLRL

Study Number 1

Lesson Eleven
The Closed Roll

The "Closed Roll," or "Rudimental Roll," is played by using a single hand stroke that incorporates an "open-close" motion. Think of throwing the stick at the drum. As the stick strikes the drum, slightly open your hand to allow the stick to bounce then quickly close it to produce the bounce and snap the stick back in to position to make the next stroke. Remember, you are making only one hand motion. Make a "bubba" sound.

The Closed Roll Exercise

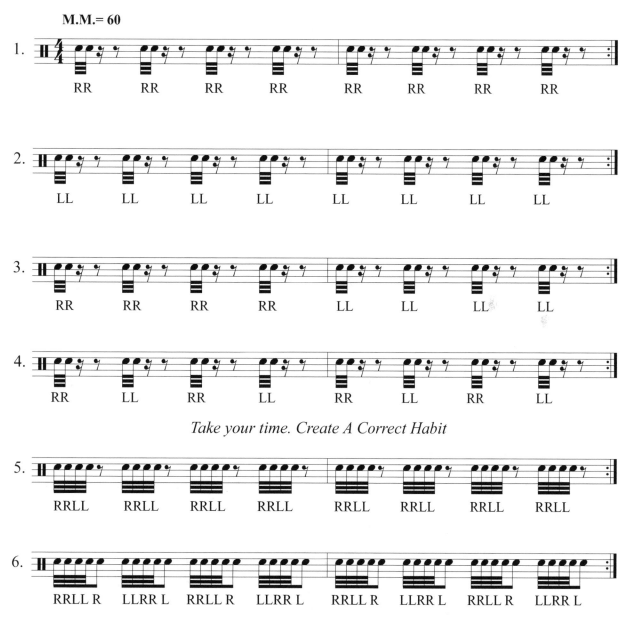

Take your time. Create A Correct Habit

This is the five stroke roll. Note that it alternates sticking when played in the rudimental style. Follow the General Rule For Sticking when playing in the concert style.

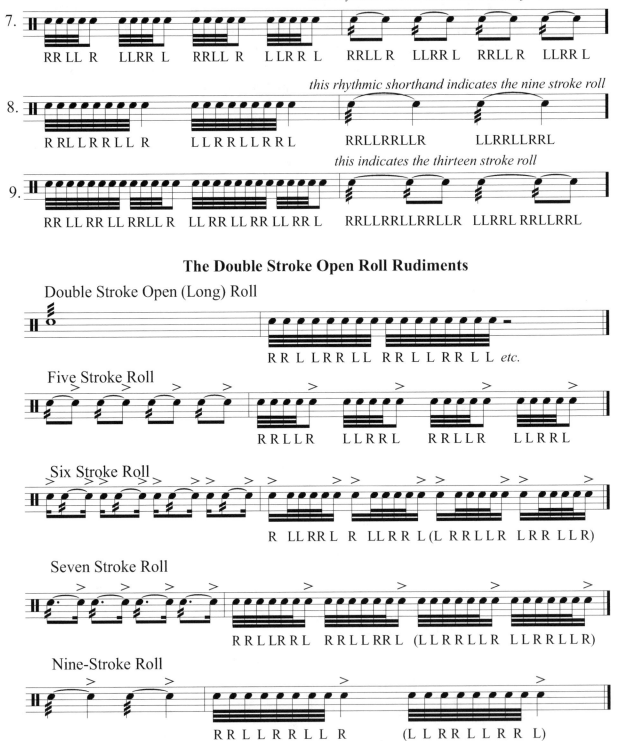

this rhythmic shorthand indicates the five stroke roll

7.

RR LL R   LLRR L   RRLL R   LL R R L   RRLL R   LLRR L   RRLL R   LLRR L

this rhythmic shorthand indicates the nine stroke roll

8.

R RL L R R LL R   LL R R LL R R L   RRLLRRLLR   LLRRLLRRL

this indicates the thirteen stroke roll

9.

RR LL RR LL RRLL R   LL RR LL RR LL RR L   RRLLRRLLRRLLR   LLRRL RRLLRRL

The Double Stroke Open Roll Rudiments

Double Stroke Open (Long) Roll

R R L L RR L LL   RR L L RR LL *etc.*

Five Stroke Roll

RRLLR   LLRRL   RRLLR   LLRRL

Six Stroke Roll

R LLRRL R LLRR L (L RRLLR L RR LLR)

Seven Stroke Roll

RRLLRRL RRLLRRL (LLRRLLR LLRRLLR)

Nine-Stroke Roll

R R L L R R L L R   (L L R R L L R R L)

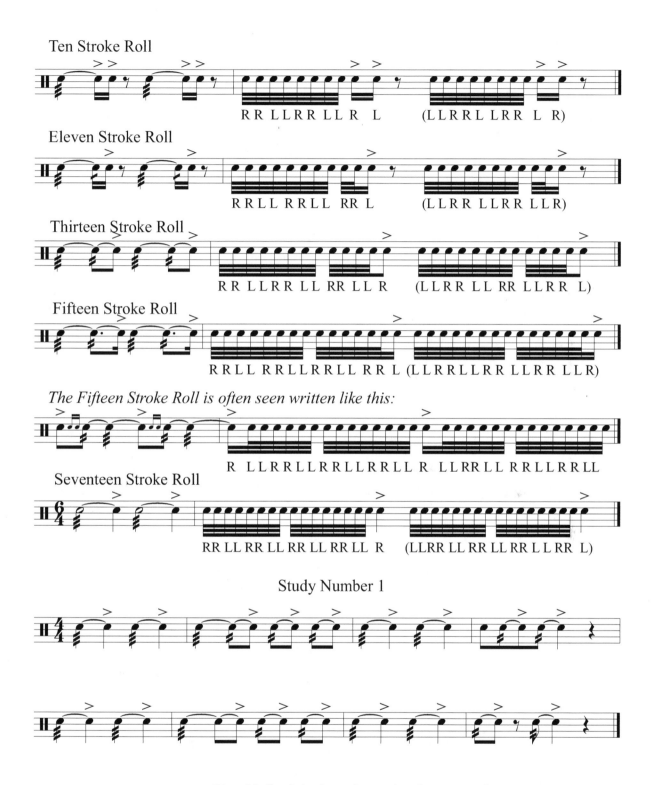

Ten Stroke Roll

R R L L R R L L R   L   (L L R L L R R   L   R)

Eleven Stroke Roll

R R L L R R L L R R L   (L L R L L R R L L R)

Thirteen Stroke Roll

R R L L R R L L R R L L R   (L L R R L L R R L L R R   L)

Fifteen Stroke Roll

R R L L R R L L R R L L R R L (L L R L L R R L L R R L L R)

The Fifteen Stroke Roll is often seen written like this:

R L L R R L L R R L L R R L L R   L L R R L L R R L L R R L L

Seventeen Stroke Roll

R R L L R R L L R R L L R R L L R   (L L R R L L R R L L R R L L R R   L)

Study Number 1

Play this Study in the rudimental and concert styles.

The Triple Stroke Roll

Here are two exercises that will not only improve your triple stroke roll, but your double stroke and single stroke as well! Use the open-close hand technique to do these exercises.

Open your hand after the first note (slightly; don't take your fingers off the stick) to get the second note (a rebound) and close your hand to snap the third note. Be sure to keep the triplet consistent.

Creating a correct habit of finger control will not only improve your facility on drum heads, but on fast ride cymbal and closed hi-hat patterns in all styles of music.

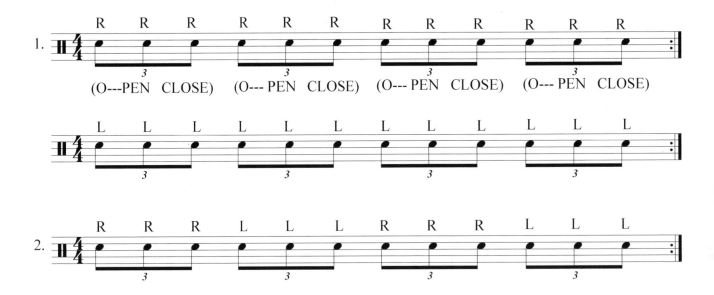

Play each exercise many times at different dynamic levels. Keep your muscles relaxed. Be sure to use The Three Ps so that you are not choking the stick. Work for speed and rhythmic consistency.

Lesson Twelve
Introducing The Drag

The drag is very much like the flam; the difference is that it has two grace notes played before a note instead of one. We use the same "Set-Switch" technique to play the drag as we used for the flam. We use the bounced stroke to produce the grace notes. Again, grace notes are played close to the drum. Put your hands in the "set" position. To play a drag, "switch" hand positions, moving <u>both hands at the same time</u>. Your hands will then be "set" for the next drag.

Be sure to play the grace notes as closely as possible to the main note.

Study Number 1

* The composer will usually display a "courtesy time signature" at the end of a line as a warning that you are going to suddenly change time signatures.

The Remaining Drag Rudiments

Single Drag Tap

Double Drag Tap

Lesson 25

Single Dragadiddle

Drag Paradiddle #1

Drag Paradiddle #2

Single Ratamacue

Double Ratamacue

Triple Ratamacue

Lesson Thirteen
Introducing The Ruff

The ruff and the drag are often confused with each other. This is because composers usually don't make an indication of sticking; they leave that to the performer.

Technically and traditionally speaking, the grace notes in a drag are bounced and the grace notes in a ruff are single strokes. Historically, what we now call a drag was known as a "half-drag." The drag was known and played as what we now call the "single-drag tap." The double-drag that is in our modern list of rudiments was a "double-drag tap."

There can be, of course, points of contention with this interpretation of our drumming heritage. For our purposes, however, drags are bounced and ruffs are single strokes. We must be prepared to play whatever the music requires.

Three-Stroke Ruff

RLR   RLR   RLR   RLR

Four-Stroke Ruff (Single-Stroke Four)

LRLR   LRLR   LRLR   LRLR

Five-Stroke Ruff

RLRLR   RLRLR   RLRLR   RLRLR

Seven-Stroke Ruff (Single-Stroke Seven)

RLRLRLR   RLRLRLR   RLRLRLR   RLRLRLR

All of these stickings are arranged so that the main note is played with the right hand.
With the exception of the four-stroke ruff, you may alternate the sticking for the rudimental style.

Call it a drag or ruff, when we see these rhythms we should be prepared for either sticking.

RLR   LRL   LRLR   RLRL   RLRLR   LRLRL   RLRLRLR   LRLRLRL

LLR   RRL   LLLR   RRRL   RRLLR   LLRRL   RRLLRRL   LLRRLLR

36

Study No. 1

Practice this Study slowly and carefully.
Make sure that your drum has a crisp snare sound.

Control and Endurance Exercises

Be careful not to accent any notes   Keep your sticks at the same height

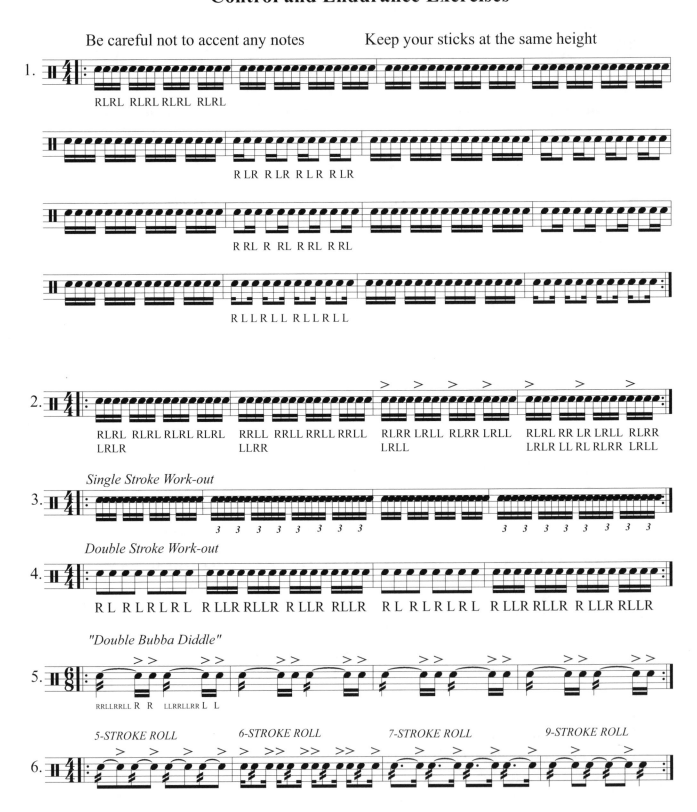

38

First Etude

Moderate March Tempo

Second Etude

Third Etude

March Tempo in the rudimental style

Fourth Etude

Fourth Etude

43

Fifth Etude

Sixth Etude

PROPER FUNDAMENTALS FOR DRUM SET

TABLE OF CONTENTS

Practice Tips

"To achieve great things, two things are needed: a plan, and not quite enough time."
Leonard Bernstein (1918-1990)

It is very important that you practice your music skills every day. Having a regular time in a prepared area will really help create a good practice routine. Choose a time for your practice that minimizes interruptions. Keeping your mind focused on the work at hand helps to create correct habits. Creating correct habits requires daily attention.

Your practice area should have your drums, metronome/drum machine, method books/sheet music, sticks, music stand, pencils, and CD/MP3 Player in place. The area should be properly lit with a relatively constant temperature and humidity. This is best for your drums and yourself. Keep the area free from distractions.

It is important to take good care of your drums. Make sure that they are tuned properly. Besides the fact that they will sound better, they will also provide a better playing surface and proper tensioning will help the shells to stay round.

Suggestions For a Good Practice Session

"You cannot be disciplined in great things and undisciplined in small things."
General George S. Patton (1885-1945)

Start with Rudiments. Practicing Single and Double Stroke Rolls and the Flam Rudiments is not only necessary to develop technical facility, it also helps to stretch and warm up your hands and wrists.

Next, apply these Rudiments to the total drum set. Make sure that your drums and cymbals are at the best height and angle to ensure proper stick contact with the playing surface. Don't forget to use your feet for time keeping or as part of a Rudiment.

When starting a new piece of music use the HOWL Method:
H is for <u>Hack</u>. You are going to "hack your way through" this piece. Don't stop; try to make mental notes of problem areas as you proceed to the end of the piece. This helps us to practice sight-reading.

Being able to play a piece at sight is a required skill for a complete musician. Gaining practice at sight reading is difficult, because once you have read a piece you can't sight-read it again. Take advantage of any opportunity to practice sight-reading.

O is for <u>Observe</u>. Look over the work you have just done. Find the problem areas. Did you miss a dynamic marking or a repeat sign? Was one measure or section confusing?

W is for <u>Write</u>. Take your pencil and make small markings that will help you in your performance of this piece. Perhaps circling a repeat sign or dividing a measure into single beats will help you to learn the piece. Sticking is very important to a consistent performance. Note the starting hand and notate a double sticking if necessary. Don't mark your music too much or it will become confusing.

L is for <u>Learn</u>. We learn through repetition. You are now prepared to learn this piece by creating correct habits. If you need to isolate one measure or a small area that is giving you trouble HOWL at it again! Do what you need to create a correct habit.

Remember why you wanted to become a drummer. Whatever the reason, keep that love and excitement. Don't let your practice session become a chore. Play some music that you like as well as try something new or play a beat you just heard on the radio. Set your metronome and chart your progress on some rudiments.

Never forget that you are part of a wonderful brotherhood. We number in the millions, we date back thousands of years, we are an important part of world history, we come in many sizes, colors, faiths, and abilities, and we are all part of one family.

You owe it to the art of music, everyone who has ever played the instrument, and to yourself to always give your best effort.

The more you improve as a musician the greater your love for music will be. Enjoy!

I do not agree with the old saying, "Practice makes perfect!" Practice doesn't make perfect, it makes <u>better</u>. We practice to create a correct habit.

Rock Drumming

Be sure to count out loud.

RIDE CYMBAL
SNARE DRUM
BASS DRUM
HI-HAT

2.

3.

4.

5.

PLAY THE BASS DRUM LIKE YOU PLAY THE SNARE DRUM; DON'T LEAVE THE BEATER ON THE HEAD.
KEEP YOUR HEELS DOWN AND COUNT OUT LOUD.

PLAY THE HI-HAT WITH A STRONG MOTION THAT WILL PRODUCE A "CHICK" SOUND.

R.C.
S.D.
B.D.
H.H.

2.

3.

4.

5.

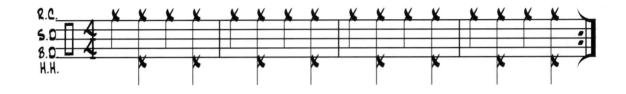

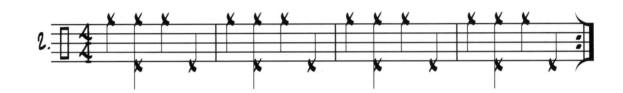

BE SURE TO USE YOUR LEFT HAND ON THE SNARE DRUM

1.

2.

3.

4.

5.

1.

2.

3.

4.

5.

54

PUTTING IT ALL TOGETHER!

Be sure to count out loud and keep your sounds even.

1.

2.

3.

4.

5.

Rock Beats With An 8th Note Ride

Be sure to count out loud

R.C.
S.D.
B.D.
H.H.

2.

3.

4.

5.

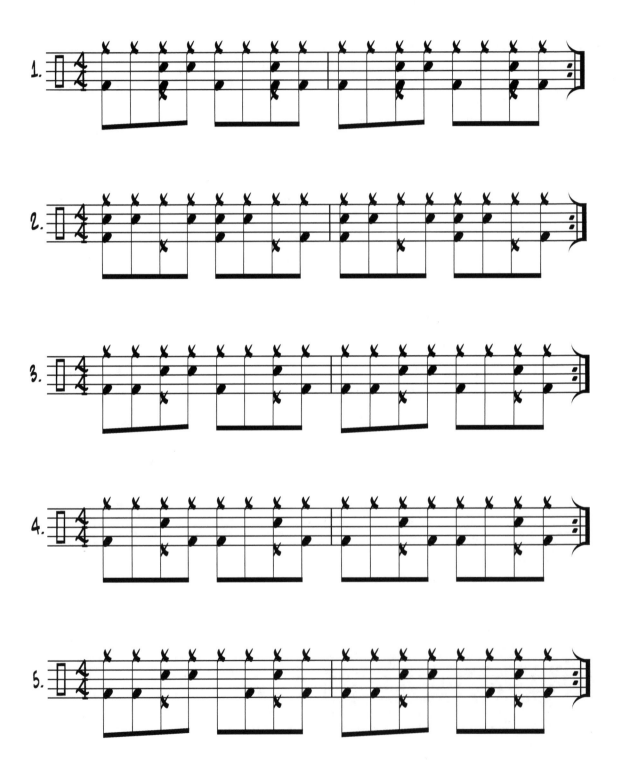

Two Bar Phrases

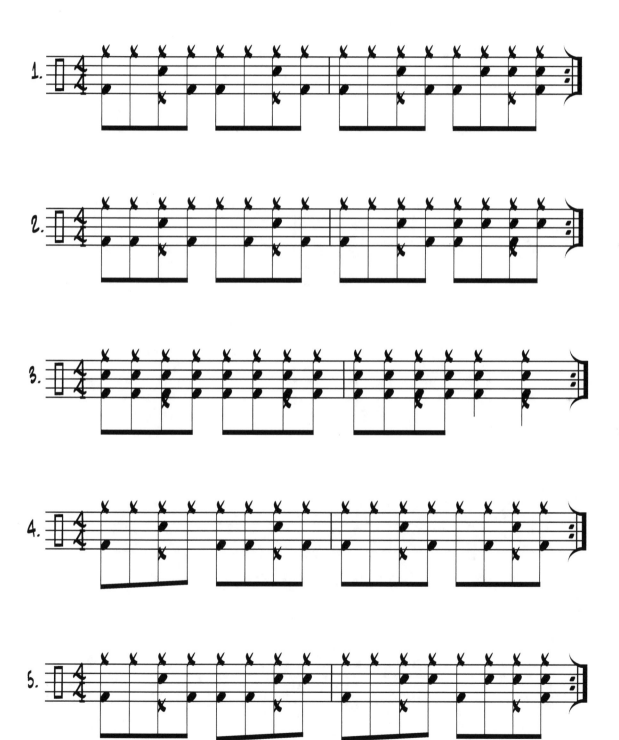

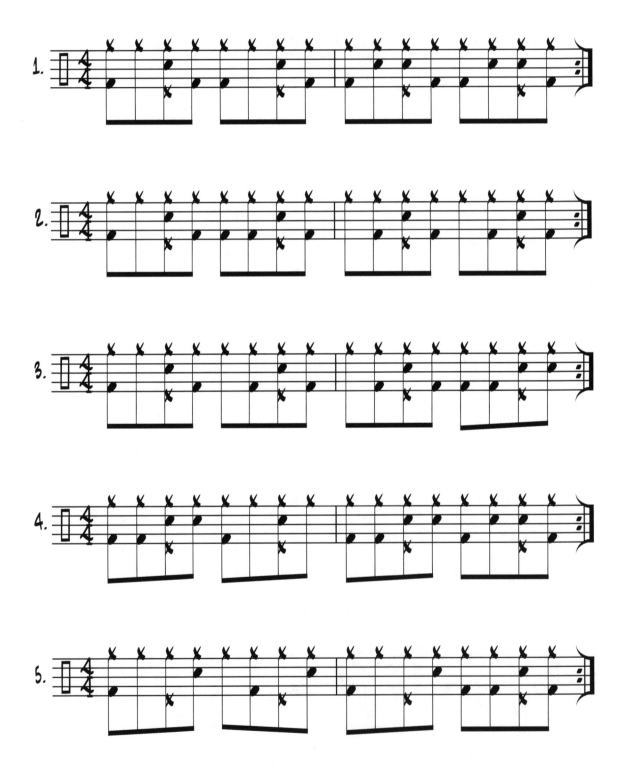

Adding 16th Notes Into Rock Beats

Be sure to count out loud

1.

2.

3.

4.

5.

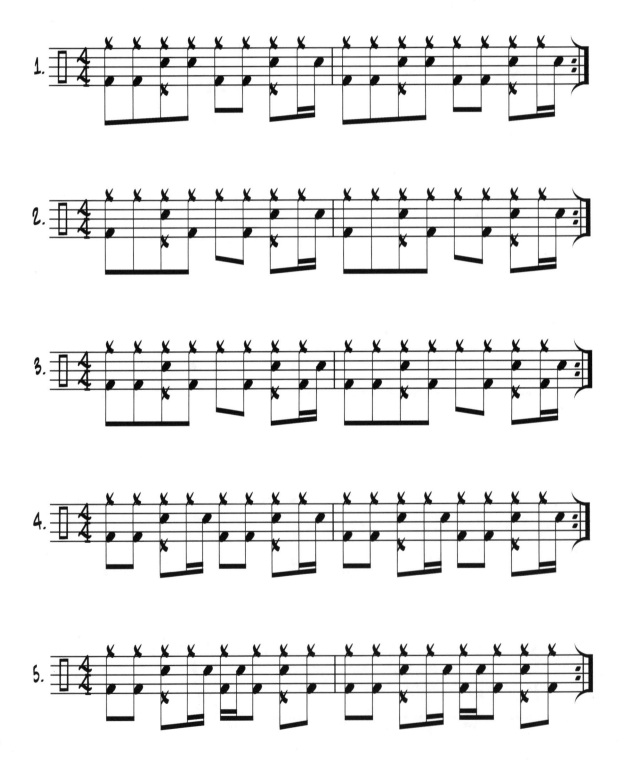

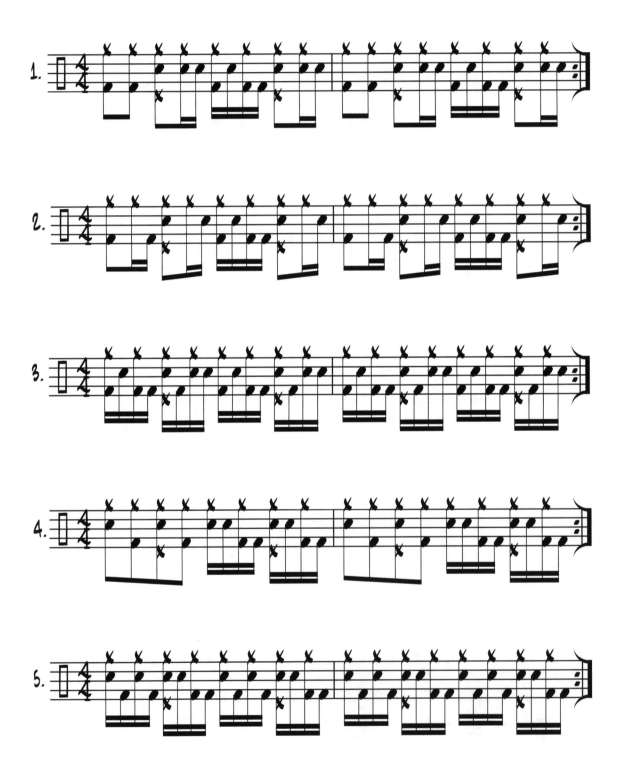

64

FILLS

BEING ABLE TO PLAY FILLS TASTEFULLY IS AN IMPORTANT SKILL FOR DRUMMERS. BEING ABLE TO PLAY A FILL THAT ADDS TO THE SONG, KEEPS TIME, AND LANDS ON THE DOWNBEAT WILL MAKE YOU A VALUABLE ASSET TO ANY BAND. THE PEOPLE YOU PLAY WITH DON'T CARE HOW MANY NOTES YOU CAN CRAM INTO ONE MEASURE; THEY CARE THAT YOU CAN NAVIGATE THEM SUCCESSFULLY FROM ONE PHRASE TO THE NEXT. WE WILL USE SOME BEATS WE HAVE LEARNED WITH SOME SIMPLE FILLS. BE SURE TO COUNT OUT LOUD.

S.T.T. IS SMALL TOM-TOM

S.D. IS SNARE DRUM

F.T.T. IS FLOOR TOM-TOM

B.D. IS BASS DRUM

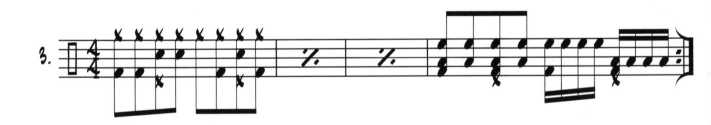

CREATE YOUR OWN BEATS AND FILLS. USE THE RUDIMENTS IN YOUR FILLS.

1.

2.

3.

(TRY A PARADIDDLE STICKING)

4.

FUNK DRUMMING

Closed H.H.
S.D.
B.D.

2.

3.

4.

OPEN AND CLOSED HI-HAT

O = OPEN THE HI-HAT

+ = CLOSE IT ON THE BEAT

1.

2.

3.

4.

16th Note Open and Closed Patterns

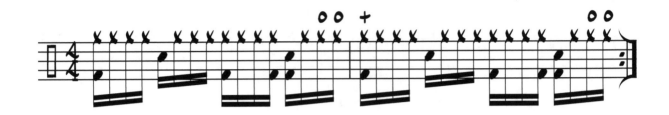

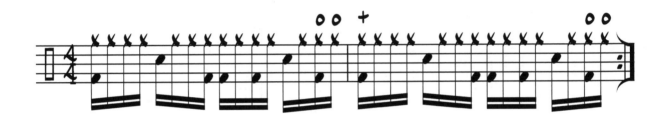

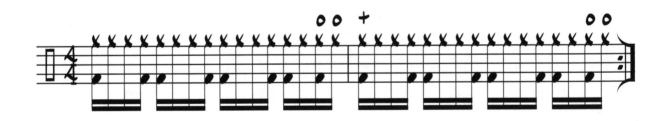

The Blues Drummer

Put simply, Blues is a combination of African and European music, blended perfectly in the melting pot of America. Most of the instruments used to create this new music came from the European marching bands. The main percussion instruments of a standard marching band are the snare drum, bass drum, and cymbals. These are also the main instruments of the drum set.

The first jazz/blues drummers were doing the work of three musicians when they combined the three instruments into one multiple percussion instrument, creating the drum set. The instruments are European, but the combination is American.
The drum set is one of America's greatest contributions to the world's music.

So, what did they play?

The early blues and jazz drummers adapted the marching band style of drumming to this blossoming new style. Outdoor concerts and parades were quite popular, so the young musicians heard a lot of rudimental drumming. The challenge was to play this marching style in a way that would not prove to be too bombastic to the melody.

First, an example of a marching snare drum part:

* The bass drum and cymbals would play together, on the beat.

Played in a 12/8 Blues, the notation would look like this:

In order to keep this swinging feel and be more musical, drummers such as Warren "Baby" Dodds (1898-1959) and Arthur "Zutty" Singleton (1898-1975) turned the flams into "Press Rolls."

As the music became more bold and expressive, the drummer took a more active part in its creation. The cymbal became a time-keeping device and not just a loud accent. The development of the hi-hat stand allowed a cymbal backbeat to be played with the foot.

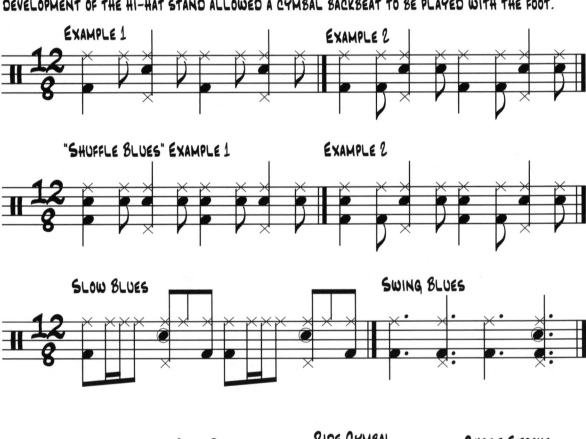

SWING

Swing is played with four beats in a measure with a triplet feel. It is important to note that Swing Music was meant primarily for dancing. The basic swing rhythm sounds like this:

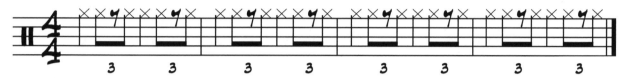

The Hi-Hat was the primary time keeping instrument. Play the rhythm on the open Hi-Hat on beats One and Three and close it on two and four to get the basic time keeping rhythm.

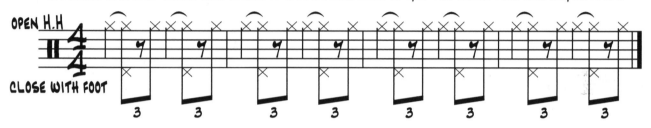

Lightly playing the bass drum on all four beats gives us the traditional swing beat. Keep the drum sounds softer than the cymbal sounds. The Bass Drum must blend with the Bass.

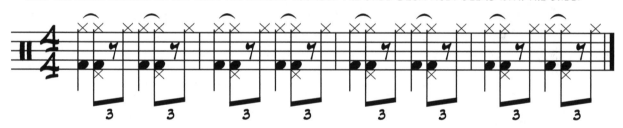

The snare drum, if used at all, is generally played as a cross-stick on beat four.

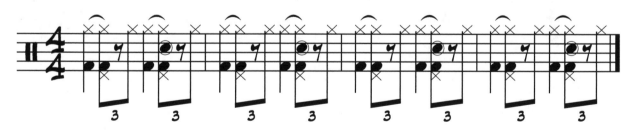

The drum parts in Swing arrangements are often a point of consternation. The drummer, to one extent or another, usually must "interpret" a chart rather than read it. Some arrangers assume this to be the case and give a chart that is more of a "guide" than a piece of percussion music. Some arrangers write out everything that they feel should be included in the drummer's performance. Let your listening skills be your guide. Depending on the arranger or the age of the drum part you might expect to see:

Or:

Or:

Or:

But, it all means to play:

BUDDY RICH (1917-1987) ON DRUM CHARTS:

"I think it's very important that you read. I think you should read in order to know what the chart is all about. But, I don't think any arranger should ever write a (specific) drum part for a drummer because if a drummer can't create his own interpretation of the chart and he plays everything that's written, he becomes mechanical; he has no freedom."

SWING IS GENERALLY WRITTEN IN FOUR/FOUR WITH EVEN EIGHTH NOTES, BUT IS PLAYED WITH "SWUNG" EIGHTH NOTES. THESE ARE EIGHTH NOTES PLAYED WITH A TRIPLET FEEL. AS CYMBAL SIZES GREW IN DIAMETER, THE 20" RIDE WAS GIVEN MORE OF THE TIME KEEPING RESPONSIBILITY AND THE 14" HI-HATS (PLAYED WITH THE FOOT) PROVIDED THE BACKBEAT.

PLAY THESE EXERCISES IN THE SWING STYLE.

MAKE SURE THAT THE CYMBALS ARE LOUDER THAN THE DRUMS.

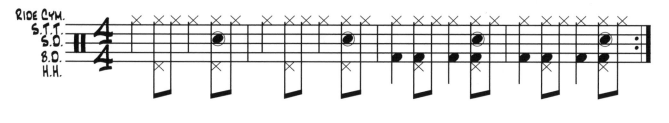

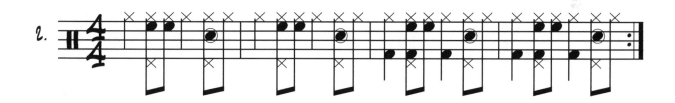

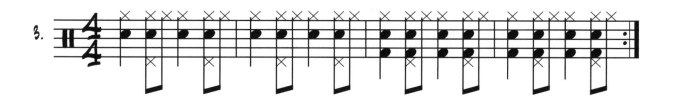

1.

2.

3.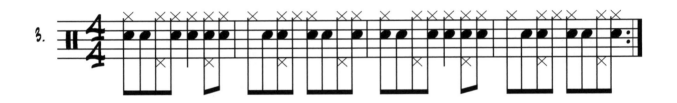

4.

5.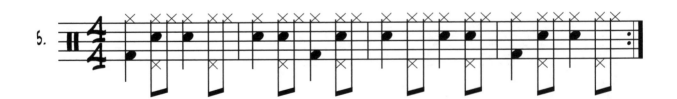

A Mock Drum Chart

(Here is the opening unison figure for the band. The figure is a guide. Which drums and cymbals you use is up to you. Use your long and short sounds to play this figure musically)

Jazz Drumming

1. PLAY RHYTHMIC FIGURES ON SNARE DRUM
2. PLAY RHYTHMIC FIGURES ON BASS DRUM
3. PLAY SHORT SOUNDS ON SNARE, LONG SOUNDS ON BASS.
YOU CAN ALSO COMBINE A CYMBAL CRASH WITH THE BASS DRUM

PLAY THIS FIGURE FOR ALL OF THE EXERCISES:

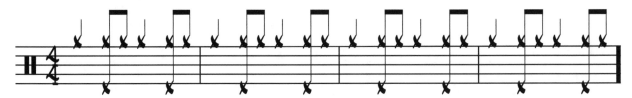

1.

2.

3.

BE SURE TO COUNT OUT LOUD.
MEMORIZE THESE PATTERNS.
CREATE A CORRECT HABIT.

1.

DRUM CHARTS WILL USUALLY HAVE THIS PATTERN WRITTEN LIKE THIS:

2.

DRUM CHART INTERPRETATION:

3.

PRACTICE PLAYING THESE PATTERNS BOTH WAYS.

TWO MEASURE PHRASES

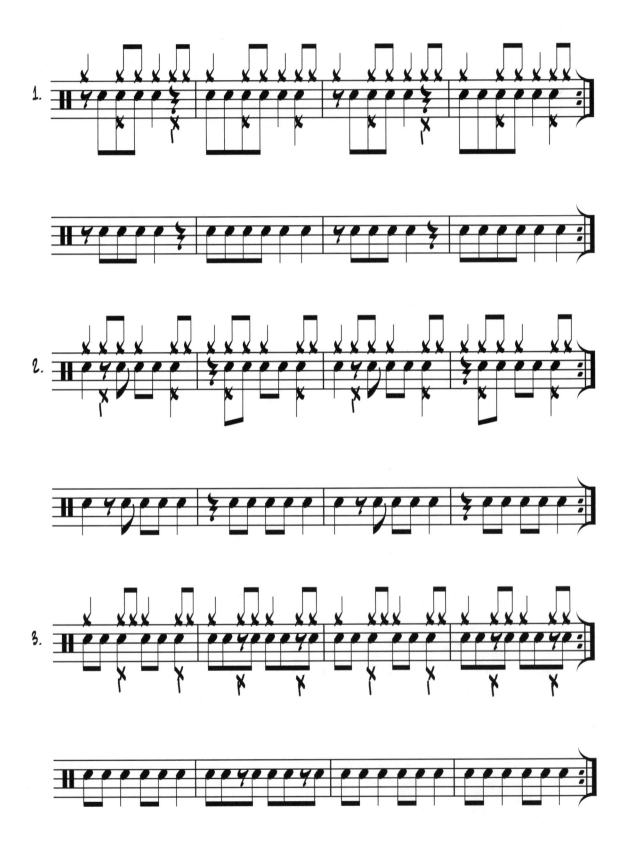

Working with Odd Time Signatures

Be sure to count out loud.

1.

2.

3.

4.

SMALL TOM-TOM

5.

Also play these exercises with a cross-stick on the snare drum

The beats in measures with odd time signatures are generally divided into two or more groups.
A measure with five beats can be grouped as one-two one-two-three or one-two-three one-two.

ALSO PLAY THESE EXERCISES WITH A CROSS-STICK ON THE SNARE DRUM

1.

2.

A MEASURE WITH SEVEN BEATS CAN BE GROUPED AS FOUR AND THREE OR THREE AND FOUR.

3.

4.

5.

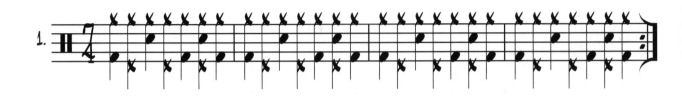

COMPOUND TIME SIGNATURES

12/8 TIME FEELS LIKE 4/4 WITH A STRONG TRIPLET FEEL. TRY COUNTING "ONE-DA-DA TWO-DA-DA THREE-DA-DA FOUR-DA-DA" INSTEAD OF COUNTING TO TWELVE.

1.

2.

3.

4.

5.

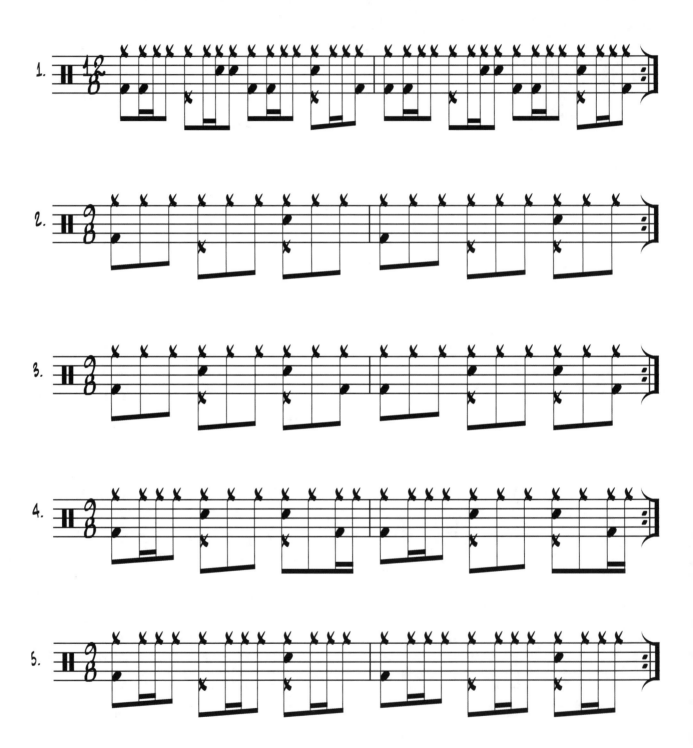

1.

2.

3.

4.

5.

Latin Drumming

The Clave (Key) is the basic rhythm for Latin-American Music.

Son Clave 3:2

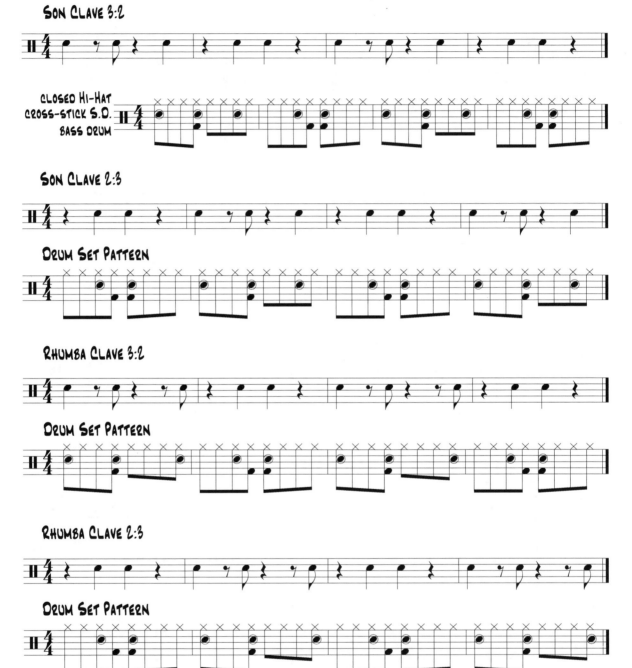

Son Clave 2:3

Drum Set Pattern

Rhumba Clave 3:2

Drum Set Pattern

Rhumba Clave 2:3

Drum Set Pattern

Bossa Nova

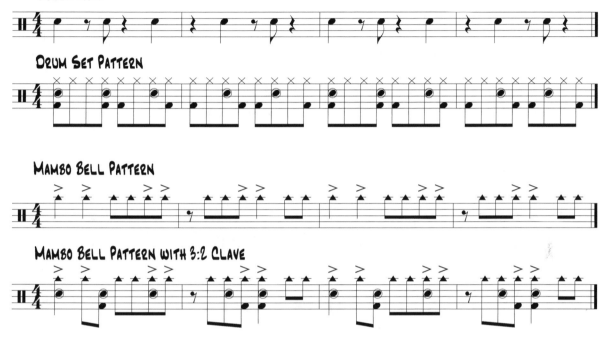

Drum Set Pattern

Mambo Bell Pattern

Mambo Bell Pattern with 3:2 Clave

Afro-Cuban (Bembe) Rhythm

small tom

The drum set is not a part of the traditional Latin Music instrumentation. The traditional Latin Percussion section includes claves, guiro, shakers, cabasa, maracas, cowbell, bongoes, timbales, and congas. When we use the drum set in Latin music we must try to recreate the sounds of the Latin instruments and their roles in the music as faithfully as possible.

The Hi-Hat cymbals are played closed, and should imitate the sound of maracas.
The snare drum is played with a cross-stick on the rim and imitates the claves.
The muffled snare drum (snares off) can imitate the bongoes.
The small tom-tom imitates the conga, the floor tom-tom the low conga (tumbadora).
The mambo bell patterns can be played on cowbell or the bell of the ride cymbal.

GENERAL RULE FOR STICKING APPLIED TO THE DRUM SET

EIGHTH NOTES SHOULD BE PLAYED WITH ALTERNATING STICKING WHEN MOVING AROUND THE DRUMS

KEEP TIME WITH YOUR BASS DRUM AND HI-HAT.

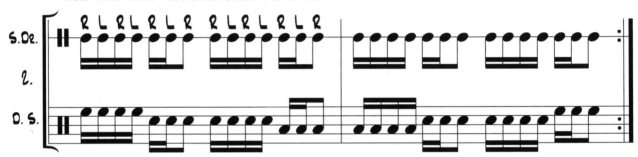

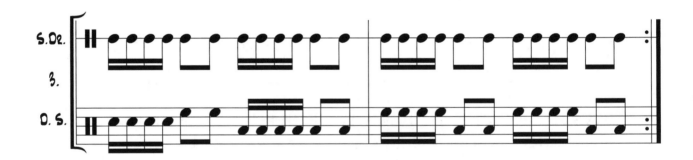

CREATE A CORRECT HABIT

Applying Rudiments To The Drum Set

Be sure to keep time with your bass drum and hi-hat.

Single Stroke Roll · Example 1. · Example 2.

Single Stroke Four · Example 1. · Example 2.

start with right hand

Single Stroke Four · Example 1. · Example 2.

start with left hand

Five Stroke Roll · Example 1. · Example 2.

Nine Stroke Roll · Example 1. · Example 2.

SINGLE PARADIDDLES WITH TOM-TOMS

R L R R   L R L L   R L R R   L R L L

PARADIDDLE-DIDDLES WITH CROSS-STICKING

R L R R L L   R L R R   L L   R L R R   L L   R L R R   L L

SIX STROKE ROLL

R   L L R R   L   R   L L R R   L   R   L L R R   L   R   L L R R   L

SWISS TRIPLET WITH TOM-TOMS

L R   R L   L R   R L

SINGLE RATAMACUE (NON-ALTERNATING)

L L R L R   L L R L R

A Double-Stroke Workout Applied To The Drum Set

THIS IS A GREAT EXERCISE FOR FINGER CONTROL. STAY RELAXED AND USE
YOUR FINGERS FOR THE REBOUND. KEEP TIME WITH THE BASS DRUM AND HI-HAT.

1.

2.

3.

4.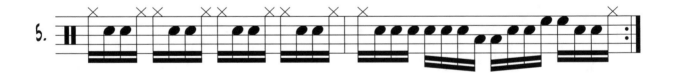

5.

6.

TRIPLET WORKOUT NUMBER ONE

Triplet Workout Number Two

TRIPLET WORKOUT NUMBER THREE

Printed in the United States
By Bookmasters